Why Si...

MW01204744

Sight words are those words that readers should instantly recognize. They are among a group of high-frequency words that compose 75% of the words that children encounter in text and use in their own writing on a daily basis. Many of these sight words do not follow standard phonics rules or spelling patterns, which makes them difficult for early readers to recognize and sound out. Children just learning to read can build both fluency and comprehension skills when they learn to read and write basic sight word vocabulary quickly and automatically.

Upon your child's completion of each activity, use the provided incentive chart and stickers to track progress and celebrate your child's success.

SKILLS

- Sight word recognition
- Reading and writing of 100 sight words
- Visual discrimination
- Vocabulary development
- Following directions
- Beginning reading and writing skills

HOW YOU CAN HELP SUPPORT LEARNING

- As each set of four sight words is introduced, write them on index cards for extra and frequent practice with your child. See page 2 for a list of 100 sight words introduced in this book.
- Provide magnetic letters for your child to use in building sight words.
- Have your child write sight words with chalk or paint them with water on the sidewalk.
- Keep a Magna Doodle in the car to practice the words.
- Point out sight words in books you read with your child.

100 Sight Words

saw	say	show	through
into	where	also	need
call	help	around	went
today	came	small	same
only	before	end	different
place	color	leave	read
live	number	word	move
play	night	does	large
back	girl	even	answer
first	school	own	early
girl	picture	another	learn
near	both	open	found
far	right	please	kind
year	mean	morning	change
great	tell	animal	off
too	old	hand	away
most	sure	house	must
each	never	world	mother
thing	white	while	tree
name	pretty	soon	present
think	follow	ask	water
until	under	turn	such
bring	want	why	write
left	try	because	walk
dear	better	high	those

Read and Write

Read and write each word. Then use these words to finish the sentences.

Word Box

saw   into   call   today

1. I like to _____ Grandma.

2. The boy _____ a bug.

3. My birthday is _____ !

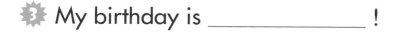

4. The bear is going _____ the cave.

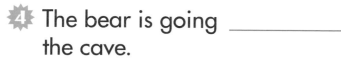 

Hidden Picture

Read and write the words. Color the shapes that have these words.

s a w

_ _ _

c a l l

_ _ _ _

i n t o

_ _ _

t o d a y

_ _ _ _ _

see		sit
call	saw	today
into	call	into
today	saw	today
onto	into	call	saw	cake
saw	into	today
	cap	sat

Missing Letters

Read and write the words. Then write the missing letters to spell each word.

only   place   live   play

1 only   ___nly   o___ ___y   onl___

2 play   p___ay   ___lay   p___a___

3 live   l___ve   l___ ___e   ___ive

4 place   ___lace   pl___ ___e   p___ace

Finish the Sentences

Read and write the words. Then finish the sentences using these words.

| play | only | place | live |

1. I have _____ one fish.

2. Let's _____ this game.

3. Here is a good _____ to eat.

4. We _____ here.

Match Up

Draw a line to match each word to its word shape boxes. Write the words in the boxes. Use these words to finish the sentences.

friend •

back •

first •

near •

1. Come _____ little cookie boy!

2. We are in _____ grade.

3. Can I sit _____ the door?

4. This is my good _____ .

Maze

Help the butterfly get to the garden. Color the flowers that have the words from the Word Box.

near	back	friend	first

near   friend   back   first

first   friend   next   five   both

bat   back   near   fast   blue

   friend   first   duck   give

Building Blocks

Read and trace each word. Then write the missing letters to complete the words.

_ _ _ _	_ _ _ _ _
f _ _	g _ _ _ _
far	great
far	**great**

_ _ _ _ _	_ _ _ _
y _ _ _	t _ _
year	too
year	**too**

Scrambled Sentences

Rewrite the scrambled sentences. Circle the word from the Word Box in each sentence.

Word Box

great	too	year	far

1 cake we May too? have

---

2 days. year 365 One is

---

3 run far. can She

---

4 great is work! This

Read and Write

Read and write each word. Then use these words to finish the sentences.

Word Box

each   thing   most   name

1 Which bag has the _____ ?

2 I have read _____ book.

3 What is this _____ ?

4 My _____ is Ben.

Ben

Hidden Picture

Read and write the words. Color the shapes that have these words.

e a c h

t h i n g

_ _ _ _ _

_ _ _ _ _

m o s t

n a m e

_ _ _ _ _

_ _ _ _ _

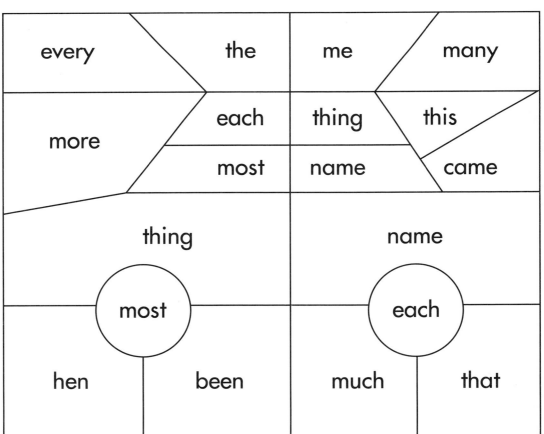

Missing Letters

Read and write the words. Then write the missing letters to spell each word.

think   until   bring   left

1 think   t___i___k   thi___k   ___ ___ink

2 bring   ___ring   br___ ___g   b___ing

3 left   l___ft   ___eft   lef___

4 until   ___ntil   unt___l   u___til

Scrambled Words

Read and write the words. Unscramble the letters
in each box to make words to finish the sentences.

u n t i l

l e f t

___ ___ ___ ___ ___

___ ___ ___ ___

t h i n k

b r i n g

___ ___ ___ ___ ___

___ ___ ___ ___ ___

| h i k |
| t n |

What do you _____
about my new pet?

| t l |
| i u ⁿ |

I cannot go _____ I
get my book.

| f t |
| e l |

There is one cookie _____.

| g b |
| n i r |

Can you _____ me
my lunch?

Match Up

Draw a line to match each word to its word shape boxes. Write the words in the boxes. Use these words to finish the sentences.

dear

say

where

help

1 _____ did the dog go?

2 I can _____ my ABCs!

3 She is a _____ friend.

4 I can _____ you with that.

Maze

Help the dog get to the doghouse. Color the paw prints that have the words from the Word Box.

Word Box

| say | dear | help | where |

dear	help	where	say
met	do	here	why	where
day	help	say	dear	help
near	where	then	day	thing
the	help	dear	say

Building Blocks

Read and trace each word. Then write the missing letters to complete the words.

------

c _ _ _ _ _

color

color

------

b _ _ _ _ _ _

before

before

------

n _ _ _ _ _ _

number

number

------

c _ _ _ _

came

came

Scrambled Sentences

Rewrite the scrambled sentences. Circle the word from the Word Box in each sentence.

1 number   This   the   ten.   is

_____

_____

2 with   dog   came   My   me.

_____

_____

3 like?   color   What   you   do

_____

_____

4 before   Eat   your   apple   you   go.

_____

_____

© 2012 CTP - 7224

Read and Write

Read and write each word. Then use these words to finish the sentences.

Word Box

night   girl   school   picture

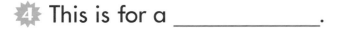

1 I sleep at _____ .

2 This is a _____
of a frog.

3 We go to _____ .

4 This is for a _____ .

Read, Write, Choose

Read and write the words. Then fill in the bubble next to the correct word for each sentence.

s c h o o l   n i g h t

___ ___ ___ ___ ___ ___   ___ ___ ___ ___ ___

g i r l   p i c t u r e

___ ___ ___ ___   ___ ___ ___ ___ ___ ___ ___

1 I see the _____.

ⓐ gril   ⓑ girl   ⓒ gil

2 We sleep at _____.

ⓐ night   ⓑ nite   ⓒ nght

3 Do you go to _____?

ⓐ skool   ⓑ scool   ⓒ school

4 I made this _____.

ⓐ pitchur   ⓑ picture   ⓒ picher

20

Missing Letters

Read and write the words. Then write the missing letters to spell each word.

both   right   mean   tell

1. both   ___oth   b___th   bo___ ___

2. mean   m___an   me___n   ___ean

3. right   ri___ ___t   ___ight   r___gh___

4. tell   t___ll   ___ell   te___l

Scrambled Words

Read and write the words. Unscramble the letters in each box to make words to finish the sentences.

t e l l

m e a n

___ ___ ___ ___

___ ___ ___ ___

r i g h t

b o t h

___ ___ ___ ___ ___

___ ___ ___ ___

| o b
h t | I like _____ bears. |

| l e
t l | I will _____ them hello. |

| i h
g t r | This is my _____ hand. |

| e m
n a | Here is a _____ wolf. |

Match Up

Draw a line to match each word to its word shape boxes. Write the words in the boxes. Use these words to finish the sentences.

old •

sure •

never •

white •

1 Are you _____ about that?

2 He has a _____ hat.

3 The _____ man is my grandpa.

DANGER STAY OUT

4 We _____ go there.

© 2012 CTP - 7224

23

Hidden Picture

Read and write the words. Color the shapes that have these words.

s u r e

_ _ _ _

white

_ _ _ _ _

o l d

_ _ _

n e v e r

_ _ _ _ _

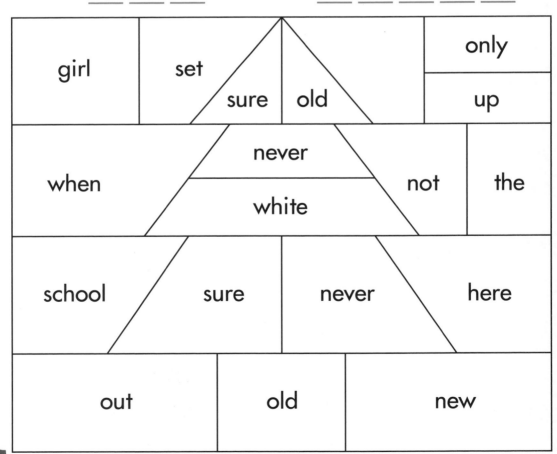

Building Blocks

Read and trace each word. Then write the missing letters to complete the words.

_____	_____
p_____	u_____
pretty	under
pretty	**under**

_____	_____
w___	f_____
want	follow
want	**follow**

Scrambled Sentences

Rewrite the scrambled sentences. Circle the word from the Word Box in each sentence.

Word Box

pretty   follow   under   want

1 I   pretty   have   flowers.

---

2 you   this?   Do   want

---

3 me   Follow   the   park.   to

---

4 ball   the   under   The   is   tree.

Read and Write

Read and write each word. Then use these words to finish the sentences.

Word Box

try	show	also	better

1. Let's _____ to win the game!

2. I can hear you _____ now.

3. Will you _____ me your new backpack?

4. I _____ need eggs to make cookies.

Maze

Help the bird get to the nest in the tree. Color the cloud shapes that have the words from the Word Box.

try	better	show	also

better   also   try

try   they   after   she

show   also   better   try

always   tell   shell   show

better   show   also

Missing Letters

Read and write the words. Then write the missing letters to spell each word.

around   small   end   leave

1 around   aro____nd   a____ou____d   ____roun____

2 small   s____all   sm____ll   sma____ ____

3 end   ____nd   e____d   en____

4 leave   ____eave   l____ ____ve   leav____

© 2012 CTP - 7224

Finish the Sentences

Read and write the words. Then finish the sentences using these words.

Word Box

around   small   end   leave

❶ This is the ___ ___ ___ of my book.

❷ The hat is too ___ ___ ___ ___ ___ for her.

❹ We will ___ ___ ___ ___ ___ at 8 o'clock.

❹ Do you live ___ ___ ___ ___ ___ ___ here?

Match Up

Draw a line to match each word to its word shape boxes. Write the words in the boxes. Use these words to finish the sentences.

word •

does •

even •

own •

1 These are _____ numbers.

2 The cat _____ like fish.

3 Can you spell this _____ ?

bear

4 Do you _____ this wallet?

Hidden Picture

Read and write the words. Color the shapes that have these words.

w o r d

_ _ _ _

d o e s

_ _ _ _

e v e n

_ _ _ _

o w n

_ _ _

into · end · do · see · will

even

does

word · even

who

out

does · own

word

what · who · did

Building Blocks

Read and trace each word. Then write the missing letters to complete the words.

__ __ __ __ __ __

p__ __ __ __ __

please

please

__ __ __ __ __ __ __

m__ __ __ __ __ __

morning

morning

__ __ __ __ __ __ __

a__ __ __ __ __ __

another

another

__ __ __ __

o__ __ __

open

open

Scrambled Sentences

Rewrite the scrambled sentences. Circle the
word from the Word Box in each sentence.

another   please   open   morning

1 door   The   open.   is

_____

2 pick   your   Please   up   socks.

_____

3 woke   I   late   up   morning.   this

_____

4 one?   have   I   another   May

_____

Read and Write

Read and write each word. Then use these words to finish the sentences.

Word Box

animal   hand   house   world

1. They live in an orange _____ .

2. Our _____ is the earth.

3. He shook my _____ when I met him.

4. What _____ lives here?

Read, Write, Choose

Read and write the words. Then fill in the bubble
next to the correct word for each sentence.

h a n d   h o u s e

___ ___ ___ ___   ___ ___ ___ ___ ___

w o r l d   a n i m a l

   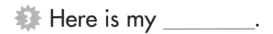

1 This is our _____.

ⓐ world   ⓑ werld   ⓒ whirl

2 A _____ has five fingers.

ⓐ hind   ⓑ hand   ⓒ heard

3 Here is my _____.

ⓐ hous   ⓑ hows   ⓒ house

4 This _____ is a rabbit.

ⓐ aminal   ⓑ animal   ⓒ anamal

Missing Letters

Read and write the words. Then write the missing letters to spell each word.

Word Box

while   soon   ask   turn

1 while   wh____le   w____ile   ____hile

2 soon   ____oon   s____on   soo____

3 ask   ____sk   a____k   as____

4 turn   t____rn   tur____   ____urn

Finish the Sentences

Read and write the words. Then finish the sentences using these words.

turn	soon	ask	while

1 Can you _____ _____ _____ your mom to make pizza?

2 I will _____ _____ _____ _____ on the water.

3 We can talk _____ _____ _____ _____ _____ we walk.

4 _____ _____ _____ _____ it will be summer!

38

Match Up

Draw a line to match each word to its word shape boxes. Write the words in the boxes. Use these words to finish the sentences.

through •

high •

why •

because •

1 It went _____ the yard.

2 My kite is going _____ !

3 _____ are you sad?

4 I'm sad _____ my dog is lost.

Maze

Help the bee get to the hive. Color the flower shapes that have the words from the Word Box.

why	when	what
high	through	because
went	through	high
high	why	there

we

bee

been

know

through

because

Building Blocks

Read and trace each word. Then write the missing letters to complete the words.

_ _ _ _
n _ _ _
need
need

_ _ _ _ _ _ _ _ _
d _ _ _ _ _ _ _ _
different
different

_ _ _ _
w _ _ _
went
went

_ _ _ _
s _ _ _
same
same

Scrambled Words

Read and write the words. Unscramble the letters
in each box to make words to finish the sentences.

need

went

_ _ _ _

_ _ _ _

same

different

_ _ _ _

_ _ _ _ _ _ _ _ _

| e s |
| m a |

These two frogs look
the _____.

| e f e i |
| d t e f |
| r n |

These two fish look
_____.

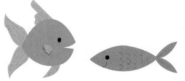

| e n |
| d e |

I _____ to eat
good food.

| t n |
| w e |

We _____ to
the zoo!

Read and Write

Read and write each word. Then use these words to finish the sentences.

Word Box

read   move   large   answer

1. Help me _____ this big chair.

2. Do you know the _____ ?

$$\begin{array}{r} 61 \\ + 38 \\ \hline ? \end{array}$$

3. I will _____ all these books.

4. This _____ animal is an elephant.

Hidden Picture

Read and write the words. Color the shapes that have these words.

r e a d

m o v e

— — — —

— — — —

l a r g e

a n s w e r

— — — — —

— — — — — —

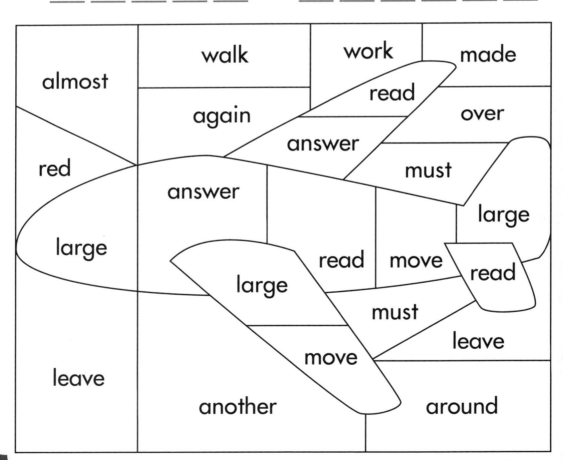

almost | walk | work | made
red | again | read | over
 | answer | answer | must
large | | read | move | large
 | large | | read
leave | | must | leave
 | move |
 | another | around

Missing Letters

Read and write the words. Then write the missing letters to spell each word.

Word Box

early　　learn　　found　　kind

1 early　　e____rly　　ea____l____　　____arly

2 learn　　l_____rn　　____earn　　lear____

3 found　　____ound　　f_____nd　　fou____d

4 kind　　k____nd　　kin____　　ki____d

© 2012 CTP - 7224

Scrambled Sentences

Rewrite the scrambled sentences. Circle the
word from the Word Box in each sentence.

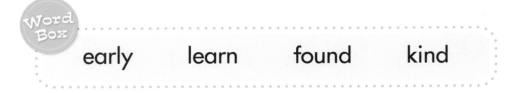

1 what   Look   found!   I

_____

2 early.   get   must   We   there

_____

3 learn   will   plants.   about   We

_____

4 be   others.   kind   Always   to

_____

Match Up

Draw a line to match each word to its word shape boxes. Write the words in the boxes. Use these words to finish the sentences.

change •

off •

away •

must •

1 Don't run _____, little cookie boy!

2 Please turn _____ the lamp.

3 I _____ do my homework now.

4 This little caterpillar will _____ into a butterfly.

Maze

Help the caterpillar change into a butterfly. Color the leaf shapes that have the words from the Word Box.

came   change   away

out   off   old   not

make   must   many   come

again   away   off   change

on   out   most   must

off   change   away

© 2012 CTP - 7224

Building Blocks

Read and trace each word. Then write the missing letters to complete the words.

_ _ _ _ _ _	_ _ _ _ _
m _ _ _ _ _	w _ _ _ _
mother	water
mother	**water**

_ _ _ _	_ _ _ _ _ _ _
t _ _ _	p _ _ _ _ _ _
tree	present
tree	**present**

Read, Write, Choose

Read and write the words. Then fill in the bubble
next to the correct word for each sentence.

m o t h e r   t r e e

———— ———— ———— ————   ———— ———— ————

p r e s e n t   w a t e r

———— ———— ———— ———— ———— ————   ———— ———— ———— ————

1 We have an apple _____.

ⓐ tre   ⓑ tree   ⓒ try

2 I will _____ the tree.

ⓐ water   ⓑ watr   ⓒ wonder

3 I will pick apples for my _____.

ⓐ mthr   ⓑ muther   ⓒ mother

4 The apples will be a _____ for her.

ⓐ prezent   ⓑ present   ⓒ prsnt

Read and Write

Read and write each word. Then use these words to finish the sentences.

Word Box

such	write	walk	those

1. I can _____ to school.

2. Let's get _____ pumpkins.

3. That is _____ a small dog!

4. I want to _____ a book.

Scrambled Words

Read and write the words. Unscramble the letters
in each box to make words to finish the sentences.

s u c h

w r i t e

___ ___ ___ ___

___ ___ ___ ___ ___

w a l k

t h o s e

___ ___ ___ ___

___ ___ ___ ___ ___

w k l a

Let's _____ to the
bus stop.

e r i t w

I will _____
a letter.

s o t e h

_____ flowers are
for you.

c h u s

We made _____
a mess in the mud.

Answer Key

PAGE 3

PAGE 4

PAGE 5

PAGE 6

PAGE 7

PAGE 8

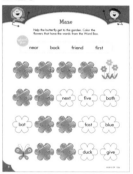

PAGE 9

PAGE 10

PAGE 11

PAGE 12

PAGE 13

PAGE 14

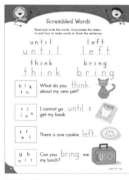

PAGE 15

PAGE 16

PAGE 17

PAGE 18

Read and Write

Read and write each word. Then use these words to finish the sentences.

Word Box: night   girl   school   picture

night   girl
school   picture

1. I sleep at __night__.
2. This is a __picture__ of a frog.
3. We go to __school__.
4. This is for a __girl__.

Read, Write, Choose

Read and write the words. Then fill in the bubble next to the correct word for each sentence.

school   night
girl   picture

1. I see the _____.
   ○ gril ● girl ○ gil
2. We sleep at _____.
   ● night ○ nite ○ nght
3. Do you go to _____?
   ○ skool ○ scool ● school
4. I made this _____.
   ○ pitchur ● picture ○ picher

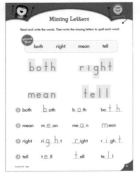

Missing Letters

Read and write the words. Then write the missing letters to spell each word.

Word Box: both   right   mean   tell

both   right
mean   tell

1. both   b_oth   b o th   bo t h
2. mean   m e an   mea n   m__ean
3. right   ri g ht   __right   ri g ht
4. tell   te l l   t ell   te l l

Scrambled Words

Read and write the words. Unscramble the letters in each box to make words to finish the sentences.

tell   mean
right   both

1. o b h t — I like __both__ bears.
2. l e t — I will __tell__ them hello.
3. i h g t r — This is my __right__ hand.
4. e m n a — Here is a __mean__ wolf.

Match Up

Draw a line to match each word to its word shape boxes. Write the words in the boxes. Use these words to finish the sentences.

old — white
sure — old
never — sure
white — never

1. Are you __sure__ about that?
2. He has a __white__ hat.
3. The __old__ man is my grandpa.
4. We __never__ go there.

Hidden Picture

Read and write the words. Color the shapes that have these words.

sure   white
old   never

girl	set		only
			up
when		not	the
school			here
out			new

Building Blocks

Read and trace each word. Then write the missing letters to complete the words.

pretty	under
pretty	under
pretty	under
pretty	under
want	follow
want	follow
want	follow
want	follow

Scrambled Sentences

Rewrite the scrambled sentences. Circle the word from the Word Box in each sentence.

Word Box: pretty   follow   under   want

1. I pretty have flowers.
   I have (pretty) flowers.
2. you this? Do want
   Do you (want) this?
3. me Follow the park. to
   (Follow) me to the park.
4. ball the under The is tree.
   The ball is (under) the tree.

Read and Write

Read and write each word. Then use these words to finish the sentences.

Word Box: try   show   also   better

try   show
also   better

1. Let's __try__ to win the game!
2. I can hear you __better__ now.
3. Will you __show__ me your new backpack?
4. I __also__ need eggs to make cookies.

Maze

Help the bird get to the nest in the tree. Color the cloud shapes that have the words from the Word Box.

Word Box: try   better   show   also

they   after   she
always   tell   shell

Missing Letters

Read and write the words. Then write the missing letters to spell each word.

Word Box: around   small   end   leave

around   small
end   leave

1. around   aro U nd   a r o un d   a round
2. small   s M all   sm a ll   sma l l
3. end   e nd   e nd   en d
4. leave   l eave   l e a ve   leav e

Finish the Sentences

Read and write the words. Then finish the sentences using these words.

Word Box: around   small   end   leave

around   small
end   leave

1. This is the e n d of my book.
2. The hat is too s m a l l for her.
3. We will l e a v e at 8 o'clock.
4. Do you live a r o u n d here?

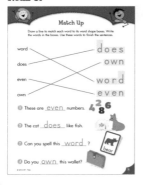

Match Up

Draw a line to match each word to its word shape boxes. Write the words in the boxes. Use these words to finish the sentences.

word — does
does — own
even — word
own — even

1. These are __even__ numbers.
2. The cat __does__ like fish.
3. Can you spell this __word__?
4. Do you __own__ this wallet?

Hidden Picture

Read and write the words. Color the shapes that have these words.

word   does
even   own

into	do	see	will
	end		who
out			
what	who	did

Building Blocks

Read and trace each word. Then write the missing letters to complete the words.

please	morning
please	morning
please	morning
please	morning
another	open
another	open
another	open
another	open

Scrambled Sentences

Rewrite the scrambled sentences. Circle the word from the Word Box in each sentence.

Word Box: another   please   open   morning

1. door The open. is
   The door is (open).
2. pick your Please up socks.
   (Please) pick up your socks.
3. woke I late up morning. this
   I woke up late this (morning).
4. one? have I another May
   May I have (another) one?

Read and Write

Read and write each word. Then use these words to finish the sentences.

Word Box: animal · hand · house · world

animal · hand · house · world

1. They live in an orange **house**.
2. Our **world** is the earth.
3. He shook my **hand** when I met him.
4. What **animal** lives here?

Read, Write, Choose

Read and write the words. Then fill in the bubble next to the correct word for each sentence.

hand · house · world · animal

1. This is our ____. ● world ○ werld ○ whirl
2. A ____ has five fingers. ○ hind ● hand ○ heard
3. Here is my ____. ○ hous ○ hows ● house
4. This ____ is a rabbit. ○ aminal ● animal ○ anamal

Missing Letters

Read and write the words. Then write the missing letters to spell each word.

while · soon · ask · turn

while · soon · ask · turn

1. while — wh **i** le, wh **i** le, W hile
2. soon — S **o** on, s **o** on, soo **n**
3. ask — a **s** k, a **s** k, as **k**
4. turn — t **u** rn, tur **n**, t **u** rn

Finish the Sentences

Read and write the words. Then finish the sentences using these words.

turn · soon · ask · while

turn · soon · ask · while

1. Can you **ask** your mom to make pizza?
2. I will **turn** on the water.
3. We can talk **while** we walk.
4. **Soon** it will be summer!

Match Up

Draw a line to match each word to its word shape boxes. Write the words in the boxes. Use these words to finish the sentences.

through · high · why · because

high · through · because · why

1. It went **through** the yard.
2. My kite is going **high**!
3. **Why** are you sad?
4. I'm sad **because** my dog is lost.

Maze

Help the bee get to the hive. Color the flower shapes that have the words from the Word Box.

why · because · high · through

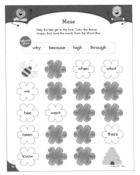

Building Blocks

Read and trace each word. Then write the missing letters to complete the words.

need · need · need · need
different · different · different · different
went · went · went · went
same · same · same · same

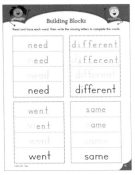

Scrambled Words

Read and write the words. Unscramble the letters in each box to make words to finish the sentences.

need · went · same · different

need · went · same · different

1. (esma) These two frogs look the **same**.
2. (efifdrn) These two fish look **different**.
3. (ed ne) I **need** to eat good food.
4. (tn we) We **went** to the zoo!

Read and Write

Read and write each word. Then use these words to finish the sentences.

read · move · large · answer

read · move · large · answer

1. Help me **move** this big chair.
2. Do you know the **answer**?
3. I will **read** all these books.
4. This **large** animal is an elephant.

Hidden Picture

Read and write the words. Color the shapes that have these words.

read · move · large · answer

read · move · large · answer

almost · walk · work · made · over · red · again · must · must · leave · leave · another · around

Missing Letters

Read and write the words. Then write the missing letters to spell each word.

early · learn · found · kind

early · learn · found · kind

1. early — e **a** rly, ea **r** ly, e **a** rly
2. learn — l e **a** rn, l **e** arn, lear **n**
3. found — f **o** und, fo **u** nd, fou **n** d
4. kind — k **i** nd, kin **d**, ki **n** d

Scrambled Sentences

Rewrite the scrambled sentences. Circle the word from the Word Box in each sentence.

early · learn · found · kind

1. what Look found! I
   Look what I found!
2. early. get must We there
   We must get there early.
3. learn will plants. about We
   We will learn about plants.
4. be others. kind Always to
   Always be kind to others.

Match Up

Draw a line to match each word to its word shape boxes. Write the words in the boxes. Use these words to finish the sentences.

change · off · away · must

off · must · change · away

1. Don't run **away**, little cookie boy!
2. Please turn **off** the lamp.
3. I **must** do my homework now.
4. This little caterpillar will **change** into a butterfly.

Maze

Help the caterpillar change into a butterfly. Color the leaf shapes that have the words from the Word Box.

change · off · away · must

came · out · old · not · make · many · come · again · on · out · most

Building Blocks

Read and trace each word. Then write the missing letters to complete the words.

mother · mother · mother · mother
water · water · water · water
tree · tree · tree · tree
present · present · present · present

Read, Write, Choose

Read and write the words. Then fill in the bubble next to the correct word for each sentence.

mother · tree · present · water

mother · tree · present · water

1. We have an apple ____. ○ tre ● tree ○ try
2. I will ____ the tree. ● water ○ watr ○ wonder
3. I will pick apples for my ____. ○ mthr ○ muther ● mother
4. The apples will be a ____ for her. ○ prezent ● present ○ prsnt

PAGE 51

PAGE 52